For A. L.

S0-BIL-347

LET NO WAVE ENGULF US

Let No Wave Engulf Us

BY

FRANK ALTSCHUL

NEW YORK

DUELL, SLOAN AND PEARCE

COPYRIGHT, 1941, BY

FRANK ALTSCHUL

Second printing, April, 1941

LET NO WAVE ENGULF US

LET NO WAVE ENGULF US

THERE are few today who doubt that we are living in a period of great historic change. Yet while this is generally recognized, the underlying causes remain obscure, and the direction and the magnitude of imminent transformation are veiled from our eyes in the fog of the future.

It is only too natural that this should be so. We are confronted with the fact of war. The duration and the spread of this conflict, no less than the nature of its final outcome, will set the pattern of the world that is to be. And when the minds of men are daily preoccupied with the ebb and flow of the tide of battle, they have little time to speculate about matters that seem at the moment of such remote concern as the motivating forces lurking behind this new threat to an old civilization.

Yet the general outlines of the new order which would follow totalitarian victory have already been made abundantly clear. With meticulous care, and with an engaging frankness, the Nazis have furnished us with a blueprint of the future. A master race will perform its God-given mission of organizing the rest of us according to its will, and within the framework of National Socialist principles. "Deutschland über Alles" is to be more than a mere battle cry. It is to become the essential core of the brave new world. Under such circumstances, we would be relieved of any obligation to worry further about our problems. These would be solved for us in Berlin, and in the German way.

But we don't altogether like the Nazi blueprint—in fact we dislike it intensely. Great Britain is now at war in order to prevent the Germans from pointing the direction of things to come. America is committed to a policy of "All-

Out-Aid" to the British. We know that this involves an element of risk—one that until quite recently we were not prepared to take. But we have at last concluded that even this risk, however great, is preferable to that of finding ourselves facing a totalitarian world alone. We are unwilling to leave to others the task of fixing the limits within which we may hand on to our children their heritage of human liberty.

As this is our fixed determination, we must make the assumption that, with a degree of participation on our part still unpredictable, the cause which we have made our cause will ultimately prevail. Yet this is far more than a mere assumption. It is a matter of basic faith—faith in ourselves, faith in our institutions, faith in a world of free men. We have abiding confidence in the conscience of men and women of good-will everywhere. We have the burning conviction that the liberties that have been achieved at infinite sacrifice through the ages will survive the impact of this new attack. In short, we have an unshakable belief in the triumph of good over evil, of right over might, of civilization over barbarism.

But it is not enough that our faith should be ultimately justified by victory. This will be merely the beginning of the task. We must have the foresight and the vision to make our own system work. We must meet the blueprint of the tyrants who think in terms of a world enslaved, with a concrete program born of our dreams of a world set free. There can be little doubt that we had all become too smug, too complacent. Smugness and complacency are poor weapons with which to face the dynamics of revolution. Unless they are abandoned, and abandoned now, we may yet lose in the aftermath of war those very values which the war is being fought to defend.

On this account, it is imperative that we in America who are still far removed from the circumstances of actual warfare, pause to take stock of the recent past. We must decide which are those characteristic features of American life we wish at all costs to maintain. We must consider how far they are threatened by the economic and social forces of the day. We must seek insofar as possible to free ourselves from the barnacles of dogma in order that we may navigate smoothly through stormy seas. We must strive to recognize the nature of the currents which are driving us in the direction of fundamental change. Only insofar as we do this will we be able to make these forces obedient to our will.

· 2 ·

The sweep of events abroad—military, naval, political—has become the chief preoccupation of our waking hours. Even those of us who as yet see in an eventual Nazi victory no direct threat to our own security and to our vital interests, are, in the main, deeply concerned and violently partisan. It would seem as if our instincts and our emotions were silently plotting a course which our reason will shortly follow.

This concentration upon day to day developments abroad was altogether inevitable. There is always drama of high order to be found in the open clash of forces. War, which calls forth so much that is base in human nature, furnishes constant opportunity for the display of its finest qualities. Under modern conditions, the whole nation has become the battlefield; and we are witnessing an unprecedented demonstration of courage, determination, and endurance by a united citizenry.

With such a compelling spectacle being enacted before our eyes, it is not surprising that we find little time to concern ourselves with other matters. Yet we should not allow our preoccupation with this tragedy to hide from us the fact that while the war may serve to aggravate and accentuate many of our problems, it is not essentially the cause of them. We must be very specific about this if we are to avoid the danger of utter confusion. It seems far nearer the mark to look upon the present conflict as the ultimate manifestation of a prolonged period of economic chaos; and it is from a consideration of this period that we must draw the lessons on which to base our hopes and plans for the future.

As we look back upon the recent past, it would seem as if we had found ourselves in the grip of forces the character of which we failed fairly to appraise. There were, of course, many individuals keenly alive to the changed circumstances of the modern world. The literature of the period is studded with the expressions of scholars and statesmen indicating a profound appreciation of underlying trends. Yet out of the welter of discussion, there arose no synthesis of national policy adequate to meet and overcome the difficulties with which we were confronted. We seemed reluctant to translate the views of the more clear-sighted into early and appropriate political action.

It is scarcely questioned that according to all the standards of the past, our economic machine

9

either had been stalled or had been creaking badly ever since the last war. For a time, it is true, we had the illusion of a return to the "good old days." But in retrospect, we can see that we have suffered alternately from chills and from fever, with only occasional and fitful deviations into anything approaching a normal, healthy existence.

It is too facile to seek an explanation of this state of affairs in the enormous destruction of life and property during the Great War. This undoubtedly exercised its influence. Yet, the determining factors must be sought elsewhere. At the turn of the century, fundamental changes in the world economy were already under way. In relation to the whole of our activities, these were still so unimportant that they passed almost unnoticed at the time. Yet they have asserted themselves with ever increasing force, until today they have become the dominating elements in the economic climate. These changes, and the failure of capitalism promptly to accommodate itself to them, appear to lie close to the roots of the underbrush in which we had become entangled.

· 3 ·

For the sake of perspective, a fleeting backward glance seems necessary. The end of the Napoleonic Wars ushered in a period characterized by great stability. With the coming of the Industrial Revolution, we entered upon an era of progress that can best be described as the flowering of capitalism. There prevailed in the world economy a general equilibrium. On one side were to be found the workshops, first of England, and later of Continental Europe and the North Atlantic States, manufacturing not only for their own requirements but for the rest of the world as well. On the other side were the great sources of foodstuffs and of raw materials, producing for themselves and for the industrial areas.

During this whole period, a reasonable balance existed between these two groups, and there was a striking development of the mechanism of international finance capitalism which materially assisted in the prompt restoration of equilibrium when from time to time the balance was disturbed. Not only did goods tend to flow more freely over national boundaries, but capital and credit, men and services, moved with little hindrance in response to the laws of supply and demand. There was a great forward surge in world trade, and the gold standard became increasingly embedded in the economic system.

It was a time when it appeared self-evident that artificial barriers, placed in the way of the free flow of goods, tended to reduce desirable interchanges, and thus to place handicaps in the way of a developing prosperity. And this view prevailed as far more than a philosophical conception, even though the United States and Germany, for reasons of their own, developed a considerable degree of tariff protection. The British

Liberal School of Economics, the cornerstone of which was laid with the publication in 1776 of Adam Smith's "Wealth of Nations," had, by the time of John Stuart Mill, taken on the shape of a solid body of doctrine which exerted a tremendous authority over the thoughts and actions of men.

By the turn of the century, there was evidence of a tendency towards increasing industrialization on the part of the so-called backward countries. This represented a threat, if an unrecognized threat, to the old equilibrium. During the Great War, a movement towards self-containment, which in a limited degree had been previously under way, became greatly accentuated. Countries which had formerly relied on the workshop to supply their needs found themselves obliged to develop an industry of their own. With the end of the War, in connection with the rehabilitation of a prostrate Europe, there was a further expansion of manufacturing facilities in countries formerly predominantly agricultural. This expansion received added stimulus from the general high level of trade and of apparent prosperity which attended the period of European reconstruction.

Coincident with this world-wide expansion of plant facilities, a striking degree of progress was evident in the field of technological improvement. Productive capacity grew far more rapidly than could be accounted for by the mere expansion of facilities. In the field of agriculture, intensive mechanization spread to the farm, and there was an increase in acreage under cultivation. This was not confined to the newer countries, such as Argentina, Australia, Canada and the United States; it extended to the older countries of Europe where, as a result of war-time pressures, and particularly because of the financial clauses of the Treaty of Versailles, the necessity of a high degree of agricultural self-containment had become apparent.

Once the post-war period of reconstruction had come to an end, a staggering investment in mar-

ginal industry and marginal agriculture found itself dangerously exposed in a world actively seeking a return to free competition and the free market. A vigorous expansion of foreign and domestic trade was essential if the burden of debts—
governmental, intergovernmental, and private—
was to prove bearable at all. Yet capitalism, in
a futile effort to protect domestic investments
which had little continuing economic justifica-
tion, asserted itself politically, and threw the
weight of its influence in the direction of trade
barriers.

There was confusion between the objectives of
government and the objectives of special interests.
National self-sufficiency, which had some ration-
ale in a world become politically unstable, was
seized upon as a doctrine conveniently designed to
stave off impending loss. Labor adopted the theory
in a vain attempt to protect employment. Tariffs,
quotas, contingents and embargoes, followed each
other in unending succession. Economic nation-
alism became the suicidal watchword. The move-

ments of capital were determined largely by fear and alarm, rather than by the free play of the interest rate. The gold standard everywhere succumbed to an attack to which it was exposed on so many fronts. And in a world of generally shrinking markets and contracting trade, the losses which capitalism had sought to avert increased to astronomical proportions, and in the end could no longer be concealed. A period of violent readjustment became inevitable, and this took its tragic toll in terms of prolonged and widespread human suffering.

A complex society is subject to the interplay of forces at once varied and tumultuous. We should avoid the danger of over-simplification. It is rash to isolate any one factor and attempt to invest it with the attribute of determining importance. Nevertheless, the role of this new disequilibrium, rooted in an essentially altered economic geography, can hardly be over-emphasized. We sought in vain to return to an earlier pattern of international trade. On every side, nations found competitors where they had previously found markets. Unable to sell, they could no longer afford to buy. The new orientation of productive facilities defied all efforts to restore an old balance. And disaster ensued.

This basic problem remains unsolved. It is for the time being obscured by the dislocations of a war-torn world. Yet it will arise to plague us anew as soon as we find ourselves once again in a postwar era. We can ill afford the luxury of repeating our blundering efforts of the past. If all that is best in our system is to have an opportunity to survive, we must find our way to a new pattern of economic behavior more smoothly conforming to the facts of the day.

· 4 ·

Another striking change in the economy, equally perplexing in its implications, accompanied the development of power production. The rapid expansion in the utilization of cheap power is a factor of the relatively recent past. It has served to multiply productive facilities to an amazing degree. Probably more than any other single influence, it has transformed our domestic economy from one of enforced scarcity to one of potential plenty. And this is a revolutionary transformation.

Much of the criticism of the recent functioning of the capitalistic system has crystallized around this development. Over a long history, capitalism had demonstrated a high degree of flexibility. It had regularly found methods of adapting itself with reasonable promptness to the gradually changing conditions of industrial and agricultural enterprise. Yet the forces unleashed by the growth of power production have still not been satisfactorily translated into terms of a workable economy.

The difficulty is of a fundamental nature. Capitalism reached its maturity against an industrial background which today under the impact of power production is in the process of radical change. In an earlier period of our history, nature yielded a meagre return for labor and effort. Productivity was low in relation to human needs. Under such circumstances, society placed emphasis upon those activities and qualities which tended to increase production. They were of inestimable value to a developing economy. They were an essential element of healthy growth. And it was in the interest of the whole community that they should be generously rewarded.

The industrious man and the thrifty man contributed to the building up of productivity at a time when this was urgently needed. In this manner they served the common good. It was imperative to offer rewards for the display of these virtues. Accordingly, men were allowed to accumulate evidences of their industry and thrift in such a form as to give them a continuing claim on future production, and in such a manner as to enable them to hand this claim on to their children. In a world in which all could not be secure, no greater reward could be held forth by the system than the ability to make one's self and one's children secure. In large measure, in response to the stimuli thus provided, the great productive facilities of today have arisen.

Out of the operation of this process, there came into being a series of instruments representing a continuing claim on a part of the annual production. These in general took the form of bonds or shares of stock. The productive enterprises on which they are based often had their origin in the effort and sacrifices of past generations. Present-day ownership of these securities frequently results from the mere accident of inheritance and in such instances has only occasionally any relationship whatsoever either to the contribution to current productivity by the owners, or to their ability to consume or wisely dispose of that to which they have a claim.

There seems warrant for the belief that we have now reached a point where, with reasonable effort, food, clothing, shelter, education and adequate medical care can be provided for the whole population. This means that a decent standard of living and a feeling of economic security can and should be brought within the reach of all. Beyond this, it means that there remains a large and varied realm of things and services to act as spurs to unusual effort and accomplishment.

The paradox of want in the midst of plenty has been recently alluded to with increasing frequency. Limitless human desires impinge upon productive facilities now adequate to deal reasonably with them. But if they are to be satisfied they must be translated into effective demand. Purchasing power is the mechanism which performs this transformation. Within our existing system the inequitable distribution of purchasing power contributes to a continuing disequilibrium. This has become almost a commonplace of our thinking. And in some measure it is due to the burden fastened upon the production of the present by claims originating in the remote past.

How this disequilibrium is to be corrected remains one of the challenging problems of the time. Government has attacked it by the sledge-hammer method. It may be that the sledge-hammer method is preferable to no method at all. In any event, it seems likely that emphasis will shift increasingly from the mere production of wealth to its more equitable distribution. Obviously the shift will go forward more rapidly in countries industrially advanced. It will follow with a lag in countries in the course of more recent industrialization. Of necessity it will be slowed down in times of great national effort such as the present, when nations are engaged in the extra-curricular activities of armament, defense or war.

Yet there will be an increasing and an insistent demand for a constantly greater diffusion of the necessities and the good things of life. This demand cannot in the end be denied. A whole people is alive to the fact that with the advent of power production their reasonable aspirations can be met tomorrow, if not today. No abstract considerations will be allowed to stand in the way of this essential human accomplishment. An enlightened capitalism must attack this problem and meet it within the framework of the existing system if it is to justify its continuing existence. For make no mistake about it, the problem is going to be met. The future will effectively resist the efforts of men to shackle it in terms of the past.

· 5 ·

These are no trifling dislocations which can be set aright by small concessions grudgingly made. They are deep-seated disturbances which can be quieted only by intervention of a radical nature. If our system of free enterprise is to be preserved, we must be prepared to submit capitalism in its recent manifestations to a major operation. It sometimes seems as if we have failed to take the measure of impending change. We are inclined to take counsel of our illusions, and we have many of them. We admit with some reluctance that higher taxes are here to stay. We recognize when pressed that we are apt to have more government in business than we have had in the past, and more than we like to contemplate. We can see that the outer fringe of what we amiably describe as the existing order has somehow lost its accustomed shape. We dimly apprehend that it is unlikely to assume again its earlier form. Yet all this represents only the most vague and tentative approach to a clear realization of the position.

We have not as yet faced the fact that after this war our system will in any event be so transformed as to be in large measure unrecognizable. We have been comforted too often by the metaphor of the pendulum which agreeably enough always swings back. This has lulled us into a fancied sense of security. We might do well to take heed of the parabolic path of the comet headed at breakneck speed into the unknown voids. For if we blindly fight a rear-guard action against the inevitable surge of events, we may yet lose in the ensuing catastrophe much of value that, with eyes open, we might otherwise have preserved.

The British, with characteristic insight, recognize this fact. They know that wishful thinking solves no problems. In the December number of that journal of conservative British thought, "The Round Table," there appears a significant paragraph:

"No one who has moved among the people during these months of tension can fail to have noted this resolve that British democracy shall be regenerated. It is stronger, of course, on the Left than on the Right. But even in the hardest-dying of conservative circles, the conviction is universal that 'things will never be the same again.' For the moment, there have almost ceased to be any reactionaries. There is no nostalgia, this time, for 'back to pre-war.' "

And somewhat further, commenting on British political thought:

"On the one hand, a marked growth of the readiness to re-examine the foundations of our society: a temper so radical as to be almost revolutionary. On the other hand, the complete discrediting of the revolutionary parties of the Right and the Left alike: a great rallying to the forces of moderation."

These words, coming from such a source, carry a warning which we ignore at our peril. They tell us in effect that a movement of the Center so radical as to be almost revolutionary is the only alternative to a revolution of the extreme Right or of the extreme Left. And this radical movement of the Center is now looked upon in Britain as "a great rallying to the forces of moderation."

Whether we know it or not, we are faced with a like choice. Yet in our country no such rallying has recently been in evidence. Party lines prevent the crystallization of a vocal Center and leave the forces of moderation with divided and ineffective support. This is the heart of our problem today. For with the exception of an extremist minority, Americans are of one mind in regard to certain fundamentals which they wish under all circumstances to preserve. Counsels of moderation still govern our thought. But because of the historic two-party system, this fact does not remove the danger that the extremists of the Right or of the Left may yet succeed in leading us down a path we have no desire to follow.

For we must recognize that the economic and political atmosphere is favorable to extremist leadership. Capitalism has not succeeded in mastering the new problems of the commercial world. Its breakdown is readily misinterpreted as the failure of a system of government. In the midst of prolonged depression, unhappy and disillusioned men turn easily to radical experiment. Leaders arise who play on the general discontent, and promise food, employment and security in exchange for the support of the people. And so, in the collapse of an economic system, a political system may be destroyed. Then, when it is too late, it develops that the promised benefits are largely illusory and have been purchased at the price of the last shreds of human freedom.

Remote as any such chain of events may appear in America today, we cannot afford to disregard the teachings of recent history. The extremists have a clear objective, they have a formula and a technique, and they have a confused and disunited opposition. These are immense advantages in the struggle for political power. Let us recognize that this struggle is already under way in our midst. Let us not delude ourselves with the thought that we are dealing with foreign ideologies which it is safe to ignore. Fascism and Communism have taken out their citizenship papers. They are apt to be with us for a long time to come. And these naturalized brands are one-hundred-per-cent-American now. Therein lies their principal danger.

The same forces which in other countries have created Communists and Fascists in the most unexpected places are similarly at work here. There is a pervading sense of the imminence of major change. The under-privileged feel that this can only be for the better. Accordingly, they turn to radical leadership, which under such circumstances, is always readily available. Individuals arise, quick to see an opportunity to advance their personal fortunes. Masquerading beneath the cloak of traditional American ideas, they become the effective agents of revolutionary Communism, hoping to ride to power on the wave of a movement aimed at the heart of our form of government.

The privileged classes, on the other hand, feel their privileges under attack. These they naturally wish to defend. Men are found who, consciously or unconsciously, are prepared to carry this defense even to a point where it involves the sacrifice of the democratic principle. They become the vanguard of revolutionary Fascism. They are

29

a large and growing company. They play on the latent fear of Communism, and like Fascists elsewhere, they seize upon political anti-Semitism as a tested weapon well suited to their purpose. Behind a smokescreen of cultivated fears and hatreds, they conceal from the people the real danger that threatens them. They hope and expect that if democracy falls, they will be able, as the members of some new elite, to maintain their privileges, even though in altered form. And this is their governing concern.

It would serve no useful present purpose to point a critical finger at individuals. It is sufficient to make clear that the desire for personal advantage expressed in terms of privilege or power is here as in other lands the usual motivating force. If this is understood, false leaders will the more readily be recognized for what they are.

Native Communists and Fascists according to a well-known pattern are already seeking to further their ends through the customary procedures of party politics. In a manner foreign to our ways, they habitually misrepresent their true objectives. Fantastic as it may seem, they may yet, in the course of a Presidential campaign, seek to convert the machinery of one of the great political parties into an instrument designed to entrench them in power. Against the emergence of such a threat we must constantly be on our guard. For should it ever succeed, the liberties of the people on that day will be destroyed.

· 6 ·

But it will not suffice to be merely on the alert. This is a defensive attitude which leads to no sure victories. Communism and Fascism will continue to make new converts just so long as we fail to revitalize the waning faith of man in the dynamism of our own system. There is still time, yet the problem brooks little further delay. Should we, after the ultimate defeat of the Axis powers, blunder once again into a prolonged depression we might well sound the death knell of our system. Nations may go down to defeat, yet the theories they have spawned will survive to plague us unless we make our system function in a manner which will again enlist the loyalties of men.

The growth of means of communication and the spread of educational facilities and education have materially increased the tempo of change. In earlier days, faced with major economic disturbance, men drew in their belts and awaited with what fortitude they could muster the dawn of a brighter day. There was nothing else for them to do. They had not yet been exposed to the well-advertised attractions of other systems dangled by skillful salesmen temptingly before their eyes. Today there is a new attitude of skepticism. Men are no longer so sure they are living in the best of all possible worlds. They have become inquiring and experimental; and they are more interested that a problem be actually solved than that the solution conform to the traditional standards of any particular system.

Great though the difficulties that must be met appear, these are in no sense insurmountable. In spite of all our blundering, the essential spirit of America remains unchanged. On the whole, we care far more for our liberties than for any other single thing. But we want these liberties preserved in fact, and not merely in theory. We realize that in some of the more recent manifestations of our system, they have become for many to a degree more theoretical than real. We know that they are inevitably sacrificed if we yield to the blandishments of the extreme Right or the extreme Left. But we know also that even under a Democracy, they may become increasingly impaired if a languishing economy fails too long to provide that background of opportunity and of security on which they ultimately rest.

This has been the history of the post-war years. It explains why in the recent past the ideological balance of trade has been running so strongly against us. Where formerly the American system was an article of export commanding ready reception in many parts of the globe, today competing articles "Made in Germany" and "Made in Russia" are not only serving our former customers, but are jumping intellectual tariff barriers in an attempt to capture the domestic market. If we are to transform this unfavorable balance, we must restyle our product so as to make it more attractive than any competing merchandise. In a word, we must make Democracy work.

If we are to do this, we must first learn to appreciate that a system of economics is no more than a constantly developing rationalization of a previously existing order. It is no mold in which human relations remain eternally jelled. Yet, when such an order in its major aspects has for a long period of time remained unchanged, we are inclined to ascribe to the laws of the system the validity of eternal truth. They have no such quality. They are essentially pragmatic and their validity continues just as long as they work, and no longer. It is well to cling to sound principles; yet the past must constantly be re-examined through the microscope of the present. In the domain of economics, the sound principles of an earlier day may all too easily be transmuted into the foolish theories of tomorrow.

The governing purpose of an economy is to provide an atmosphere in which the material and spiritual well-being of its members may be realized to the highest degree. It recognizes no obligation to accommodate itself over any long period to the preconceptions of men. It moves falteringly at times, encounters obstacles, gets over or around them, strays down blind alleys, and then, sooner or later, returns to the broad highway which leads in the direction of further human progress.

A functioning economy precedes rather than follows a body of economic doctrine. For many of our generation, this is particularly difficult to grasp. We have grown up in a school of thought which gave expression to the continuing realities of more than one hundred years. It was already gospel to our forefathers; for us it had acquired the binding force of Holy Writ. We came to wonder whether any experiment, however fruitful or promising it appeared, could be safely countenanced if it seemed even ever so slightly to infringe on inherited dogma.

Painful though it may be, we must abandon our neurotic preoccupation with the futilities of the past. At first sight this appears to be radical doctrine. It is actually the heart of true conservatism. It suggests the only possible approach to workable solutions. The "forces of moderation" still govern American thought. Yet we misread the signs if we fail to recognize that these forces to be effective must express themselves in "a readiness to re-examine the foundations of our society; a temper so radical as to be almost revolutionary."

A continuing nostalgic searching for a way back offers little more than the prelude to disaster. This is to play the game of the real extremist who sees in such a course his heaven-sent opportunity. There is no time to be wasted in vain regrets for a vanished past. The future is our urgent, our immediate concern. And in this world of startling change, we must move forward without further delay if we are to let no wave engulf us.

· 7 ·

The country has been split by violent differences in recent years. Yet the things about which the vast majority still fundamentally agree are of infinitely greater importance than the things about which they differ. It is to these things which we must cling as never before. We recognize that a system of government to which we are deeply attached is seriously threatened. To its defense we are prepared to make whatever contribution is necessary, no matter how burdensome this may appear. We are willing to envisage measures which only a few months ago would have filled us with horror. We wish to close ranks and stand shoulder to shoulder in the face of a common peril. Only thus can we meet the regimented unity of totalitarian revolution with the dynamic unity of free men.

Upon our ability to merge our differences in a firm determination to preserve those things we consider essential may rest the course of human destiny for centuries to come. The path we follow will decide whether the torch of American liberalism shall continue to burn as a beacon light guiding the rest of the civilized world through besetting dangers, or whether, in its extinction, much that we have held so dear is to be obscured in the lengthening shadows of barbarism.

This is no hysterical excursion into the realm of hyperbole. It is little more than an expression of the literal truth. Once this is understood, it will become apparent that the issue transcends all party lines. Then men and women of good-will, young and old alike, on either side of the political frontier, will seek to find neutral ground on which they can stand firmly together.

With unaccustomed diffidence we attempt a tentative delimitation of the area of fundamental accord. As an irreducible minimum, the objectives sought include opportunity, a degree of economic security, and complete intellectual and physical mobility within a body of law. The methods which it is felt are best designed to accomplish these objectives include a system of free enterprise within the framework of representative self-government, and the institution of private property.

There is still a large measure of confidence in the underlying concepts which guided the founders of our Republic. Faith in free enterprise persists for no abstract reason, but because experience has taught us that it has done more to advance the cause of human liberty and further the well-being of men than any other system yet devised. Belief in private property is grounded in a profound understanding that human rights most readily find their flowering in the security which property rights afford.

There is a passionate desire upon this groundwork to build the life of American promise rather than of recent American performance. This is pictured in terms essentially concrete. Men and women want the opportunity to work and to be rewarded according to their deserts. They wish to be able to marry in their youth, to have children, and to provide for them adequately. They want to feel that a home of their own and a modest competence are things attainable. They seek a life of contentment and dignity for themselves and for their neighbors as well.

They vaguely feel that the concentration of enormous riches and great economic power in the hands of the few is in some way related to the impoverishment of the many. They are conscious of the present tendency towards a stratification of the social classes. They believe this tendency can and must be reversed. They see nothing but disaster ahead for a country torn by the eternal conflict between the over-privileged and the under-privileged. To this, a nation of modest home-owners, having a real and growing stake in the community, provides the only satisfying answer.

Willing workers, great facilities, and abundant raw materials appear to make such an answer possible. This involves a more equitable distribution of the annual productivity, and an increasing diffusion of wealth. No rigidities of a system must be permitted to stand in the way. The dead hand of the past cannot be allowed indefinitely to weigh upon the future. When property rights have become converted into tools for the abbreviation of human rights, they enter a phase requiring the closest scrutiny. It is felt that they are in such a phase now.

The vast majority of the men and women of America wish to create a world in which they are no longer pushed about. They are out of patience with the arrogance of inherited wealth, with the insolence of pressure groups, and with the bickerings of the bureaucrats. They know that these things stand in the way of progress and that they must be brought within control.

There is abroad in the land a new and pervasive yearning for social justice. This concept, admittedly fluid, is in its broader aspects already beginning to assume definite shape. It has to do with some of the more ugly manifestations of later-day capitalism which have tended to throw into eclipse the enormous accomplishments of our free enterprise system. The fear of the more dire consequences of illness, unemployment and old age, which confronted so many, must be banished from the hearts of men. The slum areas, notorious breeders of disease and crime, which have disgraced our great centers of population, must give way to projects offering the possibility of decent human existence. The exposure of the worker to the unrestrained dictates of the employer, whether autocratic or benevolent, must be removed by an enlightened program of labor relations crystallized in law. It is much too late to argue that these are luxuries which the system cannot afford. A way will be found, for they have become part of the texture of men's dreams.

If the foregoing represents a fair interpretation of the aspirations of the vast majority of our people, it is clear that matters of difference have become of relatively small importance. There stretches before us a great middle ground on which those who place the welfare of the country above any special interest should readily meet. We are aware of the difficulties which the political system places in our way; yet we are growing increasingly conscious that these must be overcome if we are to move in the direction of orderly, rather than of cataclysmic, change.

· 8 ·

In our society, unity of purpose can only be made effective through the medium of politics. Accordingly, we are obliged to note in passing certain relevant aspects of the domestic scene. There has seldom been a time of such intense bewilderment. Party lines serve to separate rather than to unite men and women of like intent. A growing agreement in regard to objectives loses much of its potential strength in the face of an everlasting debate about methods. Meanwhile, native Fascists bore within the councils of the Republican Party, while Communists and fellow-travelers throw their support wherever it may best advance their cause.

While poles apart on many questions, these two extremist groups find themselves in general harmony regarding the foreign policy of the United States. This is no more than a faint domestic echo of the Russo-German alliance. In the defeat of the Axis, they fear their own extinction. Accordingly, we must be kept out of war. The country is deluged by efforts to foster that isolationism which still represents the honest conviction of so many patriotic individuals. At the same time, the fact is concealed that this propaganda is being made to serve a foreign rather than an American interest—that it is being used as a weapon in the hands of those who above all else desire an Axis victory.

Under the impact of this new technique, not only is the public mind confused, but the normal processes of democracy are seriously disturbed. Legislators are buried in an avalanche of letters and telegrams. To what extent these originate with the victims, if not the agents, of foreign propaganda, it is impossible to tell. The most vicious alien poison is regularly coated with the sugar of pure Americanism. And it is hard for even the most intelligent and conscientious member of Congress to remain entirely immune.

During this troubled period, the President, at least, has been in no doubt about the character of the forces abroad in Europe today. He has realized that these, unchecked, will come into inevitable conflict with the American ideal. He has not made the common mistake of viewing the war as a mere repetition of 1914 in more modern garb. He knows that we are facing the storm troops of destruction, and that their advance guard has already penetrated our frontiers. In the midst of a world distraught, he has become for millions the symbol of democracy. By this alone, he has placed us all immeasurably in his debt.

He has found a way to translate the latent aspirations of the vast majority into language so simple that all can understand. He has appreciated that civil liberties, politically guaranteed, mean far too little to men who remain in continuing economic thralldom. He has sensed the inner clash between democracy and capitalism, and has long struggled with the problems created by the growing conflict between private interest and the common interest.

In the conduct of this struggle, he has pursued methods which have fairly exposed him to attack. Yet, it would appear to serve no useful purpose to stir today the embers of past disputes. This does not mean in any sense that the loyal opposition should abandon its right to debate, to criticize, and if need be, to oppose. It merely suggests that in the existing emergency, this right should be exercised with the utmost restraint.

For upon the shoulders of Franklin Delano Roosevelt has been squarely placed the responsibility for leading us through critical times. In the discharge of this responsibility, he is entitled to our full support. For his success will be the success of the whole people; his failure would be our failure. Regardless of what the more remote future may have in store, for the next four years he is the only effective instrument through which the "forces of moderation" may hope to influence the turn of events.

On this account, it would seem that in the national interest even those who have opposed him most vigorously should, insofar as they conscientiously can, take convincing steps in his direction. They did not like the New Deal—there is much of it they don't like now. But the area

47

of criticism has increasingly narrowed to questions of method. There is little remaining desire to sabotage those major accomplishments which the country has whole-heartedly accepted. These have become an integral part of the American way. We may come to look upon them as representing the beginning rather than the end of change—no more than an early reflection of the instinctive gropings of a people towards a new and better terrain.

We must meet the President in this spirit in order to permit him to give reality to that national unity which is today so essential. A recent grant of extraordinary powers is evidence of the degree to which it is desired to strengthen his hand. The nation is awake to the nature of the emergency. We know that foreign relations are for the moment our chief concern. Yet the most conspicuous success in this field will prove to be ephemeral unless we are able to put our own house in order. On this account, our political civil war must be called off.

We should join forces and approach with new perspective the basic problem of enabling our system of free enterprise to function. If we are at last prepared to recognize that to the solution of this problem the extreme reactionaries are temperamentally unfitted to make a useful contribution, we need no longer hesitate to admit that as much must be said of the extreme radicals. Once the desire to return to the pattern of the past has been definitely abandoned, policies of the present, which appear to commit us without free and open debate to some form of state socialism, should be similarly laid aside.

We can only hope that the President may feel justified in placing himself on this solid middle ground. He would then command a maximum of support regardless of party. Upon his decision may depend our ability to offer convincing proof that our system, more than any other, is calculated to satisfy the longings of the human soul. Only on the basis of such a demonstration will we once again command the unswerving allegiance of an ever-growing following.

· 9 ·

We are engaged in a great defense effort. This, together with work for the British, is actively employing the industry of the country. Yet we are witnessing what is at best a feverish and transitory phenomenon. It reflects the solution of no major problem. The disequilibria previously referred to are only momentarily and thinly veiled. When peace, which we all fervently desire, has once again been re-established, we shall have to meet in an aggravated form the same difficulties with which we only recently contended in vain.

In all great nations men engaged in the war industries will be thrown out of employment. At the same time, there will be a large demobilization of the armed forces. Stocks accumulated for the requirements of the war will press on the markets. There will be a slowing down in many of the primary fields of production. And all this will be superimposed upon the unsolved problems of the past.

We cannot afford a new and prolonged period of economic depression. Fascism and Communism, which we find so abhorrent, will not die with the war. They flourish in an atmosphere of frustration and bewilderment. They spread like weeds in the midst of human suffering. America must offer no fertile soil for their renewed propagation.

And this can be avoided if the moderates meet courageously the challenge of the times. We must steer clear of the pitfalls that beset the extreme Right, no less than of those that beset the extreme Left. We must make representative self-government and free enterprise vital living concepts, and not merely threadbare phrases handed down from a distant past. We must once again give reality to the vision of America as the land of boundless opportunity. We must make this opportunity richer than ever before, by virtue of an awakened social consciousness. We must take full account of this awakening, and we must realize that it is not only inevitable, but that it is abundantly justified by developments of our day in the fields of industry and agriculture. We must set ourselves the task of furthering that welling desire of vast numbers of men and women to get more of the good things of life than they have been accustomed to in the past.

To accomplish our ends, the "forces of moderation" must first crystallize about a common purpose. There is no time to be lost, for we must plan for the future, we must plan intelligently, and we must plan now. It seems obvious that only the combination of wisdom and imagination of high order will prove adequate to the work in hand. Many in the past have been highly suspicious of this thing called "planning." Lack of planning, which today is the only alternative, would inevitably lead us once again along the road to chaos.

All recent history indicates that in the complex society of today workable adjustments are unlikely to emerge from the heated interplay of political life. They can only be made, if at all, through the development of a body of specific and interrelated measures, arising from a broad and sympathetic examination of our whole system, conducted in an atmosphere unclouded by passion and untinged by selfish interest.

The activity stimulated by the defense program has brought about a temporary respite which offers us borrowed time in which to undertake and advance such an examination.

It would be pure illusion to believe that any existing governmental agency has the detachment requisite for such an undertaking. On this account, it seems none too early to contemplate the establishment of a Supreme Economic Council. To such a body should be assigned the task of preparing a comprehensive program for the early return to a system of free enterprise smoothly functioning within the framework of representative self-government. This means no starry-eyed search for a modern Utopia, but it does entail a willingness to re-examine the very foundations of our society and a readiness to contemplate even the most far-reaching change.

The first objective of such a re-examination should be to devise and co-ordinate emergency measures to cushion the shock of an early period of post-war transition. The second objective should be to develop those modifications in our structure necessary to correct the more glaring evils of the recent past. A way must be found to release the potentialities which today lie within industry and agriculture. A decent standard of living and a sense of security must be brought within the reach of all.

This is the supreme task which confronts us. It is a matter of common observation that an advanced capitalism had developed rigidities which have exercised a paralyzing effect on the economy. It would not be seriously argued that laissez-faire has always served the interests of the whole community; nor could it be prudently contended that unrestricted property rights have never come into conflict with human rights. In spite of these considerations, it is felt that our problem can best be met in a manner consistent with free enterprise and private property. We are attached to these concepts because we conceive them to be inextricably bound up with human liberties. They have assumed varied forms in the past and have been subjected to manifold limitations. They must be made the servants, and not the masters, of our hopes. They must help us to realize our vision of a new America of decent homes and of contented human beings.

Most of us are familiar with the broad nature of the peace-time mission of the General Staff. In theory at least, it is constantly concerned with the task of preparing plans to be put into immediate effect upon the outbreak of war. In earlier days, these were limited to purely military measures. Today they have to do with the smooth conversion of the peace-time activities of highly industrialized nations into the most effective war effort. Upon the thoroughness with which these plans are matured, the safety of the nation may depend.

Under existing conditions, this safety may be almost equally threatened by inadequate preparation for the outbreak of peace. Nations not actually belligerent, but whose whole industry has been drawn within the orbit of war-time activities, may find themselves dangerously exposed to this threat. In our own case, it is abundantly clear that we will be thus exposed. And we jeopardize our highest hopes unless we set our course with this in mind.

Should the President take appropriate steps to bring about the creation of a Supreme Economic Council vested with adequate powers; and should he thereafter appoint to it men of high reputation, new faces not fairly suspect of being intellectually or emotionally unduly committed to any known or unknown "Isms," he might lay the basis for one of his most significant triumphs.

Everything depends upon the character of the individuals selected. To contend that men of the right type are not available is to enter a plea of national intellectual bankruptcy. They can be found in the engineering profession, in our great foundations, and in our universities. They can be found in the ranks of labor, and strange as it may appear to some, they may even be encountered in the business world.

Properly constituted, such a body would command wide-spread confidence and respect. It could approach its task in the requisite mood of complete detachment. It would have at its disposal the wealth of material already assembled by the Temporary National Economic Committee, and by other governmental agencies. It could call upon the experience and the knowledge of all citizens and organizations throughout the country. With no case to prove, it could pursue its investigations with the utmost objectivity. And its conclusions would carry great authority when submitted to the scrutiny of the democratic process in whatever manner and to whatever extent required by law.

In other countries similar bodies would be created or, where they already exist, would be materially strengthened. There would develop an early interchange of ideas representing on the economic front the equivalent of the current collaboration in military matters between the general staffs of friendly powers. Thus a problem of world-wide scope which no country can hope to solve fully on a purely domestic basis would move securely into the immensely more fertile realm of international discussion.

· 10 ·

When we have reached this point, for the first time a rift appears in the clouds. Attuned at last

58

to the urgency of change, a great rallying of the "forces of moderation" has led the way to national unity. We are planning to prevent, in a period of post-war demoralization, the loss of those essential values the war has been fought to preserve. We are seeking to give reality to the American dream. We anticipate no easy solutions, yet we shall avoid any blundering drift toward the barricades. We are determined to maintain in their integrity the foundations of those threatened moral principles on which our civilization rests.

And having reached this determination, our attention is diverted to certain hopeful aspects of the situation. Normal progress in every corner of the globe has been arrested for nearly a decade by the emergence of the dictators. Under the impulse of a developing technology, we had brought into existence the potentialities for a great upsurge in human well-being. These have recently either been held in check, or have been perverted to the uses of destruction. War, and the fear of war, have dominated the activities of men.

Once this nightmare of the tyrannies has been definitely banished, great creative forces will again be unleashed. The world is ten years behind schedule. It is eager to make up for lost time. Men and women everywhere look to us to provide this opportunity. If the spirit of America is still responsive to our great traditions, it is inconceivable that we should disappoint them.